Science Songs

From Beginning to End

A Song About Life Cycles

by Laura Purdie Salas

illustrated by Viviana Garofoli

Sing along to the tune of

"On Top of Old Smokey."

Learn how plants and animals grow and live.

PICTURE WINDOW BOOKS
Minneapolis, Minnesota

Editor: Jill Kalz
Designer: Abbey Fitzgerald
Page Production: Melissa Kes
Art Director: Nathan Gassman
Editorial Director: Nick Healy
The illustrations in this book were created digitally.

Picture Window Books
151 Good Counsel Drive
P.O. Box 669
Mankato, MN 56002-0669
877-845-8392
www.picturewindowbooks.com

 All books published by Picture Window Books
are manufactured with paper containing at least
10 percent post-consumer waste.

Library of Congress Cataloging-in-Publication Data
Salas, Laura Purdie.
From beginning to end : a song about life cycles /
by Laura Purdie Salas ; illustrated by Viviana Garofoli.
p. cm. – (Science Songs)
Includes index.
ISBN 978-1-4048-5293-8 (library binding)
I. Life cycles (Biology)–Juvenile literature. I. Garofoli, Viviana. II. Title.
QH501.S25 2009
571.8–dc22
2008038436

Thanks to our advisers for their expertise, research, and advice:

Virg Debban, Secondary Science Teacher (ret.)
New Ulm (Minnesota) Public School ISD #88

Terry Flaherty, Ph.D., Professor of English
Minnesota State University, Mankato

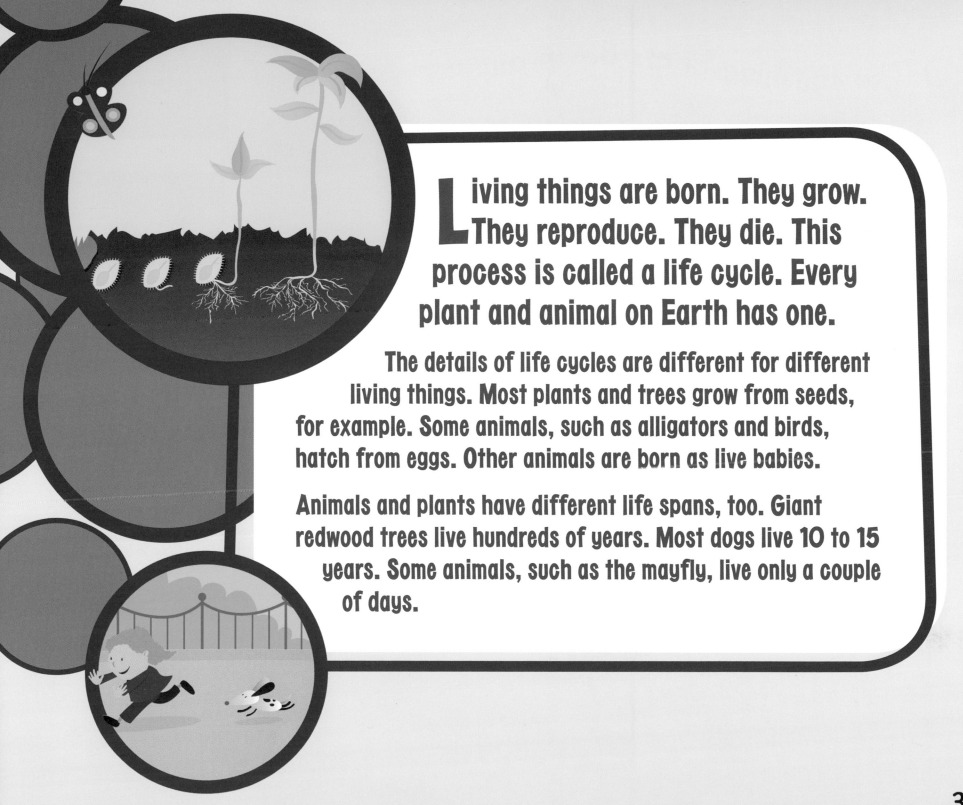

Living things are born. They grow. They reproduce. They die. This process is called a life cycle. Every plant and animal on Earth has one.

The details of life cycles are different for different living things. Most plants and trees grow from seeds, for example. Some animals, such as alligators and birds, hatch from eggs. Other animals are born as live babies.

Animals and plants have different life spans, too. Giant redwood trees live hundreds of years. Most dogs live 10 to 15 years. Some animals, such as the mayfly, live only a couple of days.

The sunshine beats down on

This papery seed.

A root grows below it.

Will it be a weed?

The rain helps it grow strong.

Oh, what will it be?

In years it will shade you,

This mighty elm tree.

Most plants start out as seeds. They grow and form flowers. Then the flowers make seeds, and the life cycles begin again.

The tree will make seeds,

The spring wind will blow

And carry them somewhere

So new elms can grow.

Plants live different lengths of time. Some flowering plants, such as begonias and marigolds, live just one year. But bristlecone pine trees more than 4,000 years old have been discovered in California!

A nest in that elm tree

Holds bird eggs that hatch.

The babies eat worms that

Their mom and dad catch.

All living things need air, water, food, and a place to live. Plants also need sunlight. Without these basic needs, a living thing cannot survive.

Soon robins are flying.

So quickly they roam.

Their mom has laid more eggs.

They have to leave home.

Large animals tend to live longer than small animals. Elephants live around 70 years. Tigers live around 25 years. Ants live around one year.

They mate and lay eggs, and

They soar through the sky.

They live five or six years,

Then one day they die.

Beneath that huge elm tree,

Sits a mama-to-be.

After nine months of waiting,

The baby makes three.

17

The baby is crying

And helpless and small.

It stays with its parents

And grows strong and tall.

Human beings are animals, too, and we follow our own life cycle. Humans live long lives, about 78 years in the United States.

Since we are all children,

We've only begun.

We have our whole lifetime

For work, play, and fun!

From Beginning to End

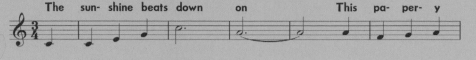

The sun- shine beats down on This pa- per- y

seed. A root grows be- low it.

Will it be a weed?

2. The rain helps it grow strong.
Oh, what will it be?
In years it will shade you,
This mighty elm tree.

3. The tree will make seeds,
The spring wind will blow
And carry them somewhere
So new elms can grow.

4. A nest in that elm tree
Holds bird eggs that hatch.
The babies eat worms that
Their mom and dad catch.

5. Soon robins are flying.
So quickly they roam.
Their mom has laid more eggs.
They have to leave home.

6. They mate and lay eggs, and
They soar through the sky.
They live five or six years,
Then one day they die.

7. Beneath that huge elm tree,
Sits a mama-to-be.
After nine months of waiting,
The baby makes three.

8. The baby is crying
And helpless and small.
It stays with its parents
And grows strong and tall.

9. Since we are all children,
We've only begun.
We have our whole lifetime
For work, play, and fun!

The audio file for this book is available for download at:
http://www.capstonekids.com/sciencesongs.html

Did You Know?

Some animals go through a special stage called metamorphosis. During this stage, the animal changes its form. For example, a caterpillar changes into a butterfly. A tadpole changes into a frog.

The largest animal egg is the ostrich egg. Ostrich eggs are about 6 inches (15 centimeters) long and weigh 3 pounds (1.4 kilograms). That's about the weight of 24 chicken eggs!

Mother animals take different lengths of time to have their young. Asian elephants are pregnant for almost two years. Opossums are pregnant for only two weeks.

Death, too, is part of the life cycle. Eventually, plants and animals die and break down, making food for living plants and animals. After a very long time, the dead plants and animals become part of the soil.

Glossary

life cycle—the series of changes that take place in a living thing, from birth to death

life span—the number of years a certain kind of plant or animal usually lives

metamorphosis—changing from one form to another

reproduce—to make offspring

shelter—a safe, covered place

To Learn More

More Books to Read

Aloian, Molly, and Bobbie Kalman. *The Life Cycle of a Flower.* New York: Crabtree Pub. Co., 2004.

Godwin, Sam. *A Seed in Need: A First Look at the Plant Cycle.* Minneapolis: Picture Window Books, 2005.

Godwin, Sam. *The Trouble with Tadpoles: A First Look at the Life Cycle of a Frog.* Minneapolis: Picture Window Books, 2005.

Kalman, Bobbie. *Animal Life Cycles: Growing and Changing.* New York: Crabtree Pub. Co., 2006.

Index

On the Web

FactHound offers a safe, fun way to find educator-approved Internet sites related to this book.

Here's what you do:

1. Visit *www.facthound.com*
2. Choose your grade level.
3. Begin your search.

This book's ID number is 9781404852938

Look for all of the books in the Science Songs series:

♪ Are You Living?
A Song About Living and Nonliving Things

♪ From Beginning to End:
A Song About Life Cycles

♪ Home on the Earth:
A Song About Earth's Layers

♪ Move It! Work It!
A Song About Simple Machines